COLLECTIONS

A Harcourt Reading / Language Arts Program

*Bright ideas
begin the
best journeys.*

BRIGHT IDEAS

Harcourt

Orlando   Boston   Dallas   Chicago   San Diego

COLLECTIONS

A Harcourt Reading / Language Arts Program

BRIGHT IDEAS

SENIOR AUTHORS

Roger C. Farr • Dorothy S. Strickland • Isabel L. Beck

AUTHORS

Richard F. Abrahamson • Alma Flor Ada • Bernice E. Cullinan • Margaret McKeown • Nancy Roser
Patricia Smith • Judy Wallis • Junko Yokota • Hallie Kay Yopp

SENIOR CONSULTANT

Asa G. Hilliard III

CONSULTANTS

Karen S. Kutiper • David A. Monti • Angelina Olivares

Harcourt

Orlando   Boston   Dallas   Chicago   San Diego
Visit *The Learning Site!*
www.harcourtschool.com

COLLECTIONS 2001 Edition Copyright © by Harcourt, Inc.

Requests for permission to make copies of any part of the work should be mailed to the following address: School Permissions, Harcourt, Inc., 6277 Sea Harbor Drive, Orlando, Florida 32887-6777.

HARCOURT and the Harcourt Logo are trademarks of Harcourt, Inc.

Acknowledgments appear in the back of this work.

Printed in the United States of America

ISBN 0-15-312037-1

4 5 6 7 8 9 10   048   2001 2000

 BRIGHT IDEAS

Dear Reader,

Do you have some bright ideas to share? The characters in this book have **Bright Ideas**, too. You will meet Carmen, who shows her friends how to make a star. Hippo has a smart idea about what to bring on a picnic. Fox has an idea that does not turn out very well.

There are so many ideas and adventures to share when you read. Come and join the fun!

Sincerely,

The Authors

The Authors

theme

I Think I Can!

Contents

Contents

theme

I Think I Can!

Reader's Choice

Shoe Town

by Susan Stevens Crummel and Janet Stevens

A little mouse is joined by many friends as they make a town of shoes!

Award-Winning Author/Illustrator

FROM THE LIBRARY

A Green Light Reader

Shoe Town

Written by Janet Stevens and Susan Stevens Crummel

Illustrated by Janet Stevens

Big Brown Bear

by David McPhail

Big bear wants to paint a playhouse for Little Bear, but he has some trouble.

Award-Winning Author/Illustrator
FROM THE LIBRARY

Mr. Gumpy's Outing

by John Burningham

Mr. Gumpy takes a boat ride with all of his friends!

ALA Notable Book

THE CHICK THAT WOULDN'T HATCH

written by Claire Daniel
illustrated by Lisa Campbell Ernst

There were six eggs in Hen's nest. Chip! Chip! Out popped five chicks.

"My family!" cried Hen.

13

One egg didn't hatch. It rolled
out of the nest.

"Stop that egg!" called Hen.

14

The egg kept going. It rolled
over and over, past the pig pen.

"Stop that egg!" Hen
called. Pig couldn't
catch it, so he ran, too.

16

The egg kept going. It rolled
over and over, past the pond.

"Stop that egg!" called Hen and Pig. Duck couldn't catch it, so she ran, too.

The egg kept going. It rolled over again
and again, past the tomato patch.

"Stop that egg!" called Hen
and Pig and Duck. Horse could
not catch it, so he ran, too.

The egg skipped over a ditch.

It hopped over a fox.

"Stop! Stop!" cried Hen.

The egg rolled into the shed and hit the wall. CRACK! The chick that wouldn't hatch had hatched!

"My baby!" Hen cried.

"Mom!" said the chick.
"What a ride I had!"

"Yes," said Hen, "and
what a run we had!"

Meet the Illustrator

Lisa Campbell Ernst

Before Lisa Campbell Ernst drew the pictures for *The Chick That Wouldn't Hatch*, she took her daughter to the zoo. Her daughter loved a horse she saw there named Lance. So Lisa Campbell Ernst painted Horse to look just like Lance. She hopes that you draw things you see around you, too!

Lisa Campbell Ernst

Visit *The Learning Site!*
www.harcourtschool.com

25

Hatching an Egg

You can make the chick that wouldn't hatch.

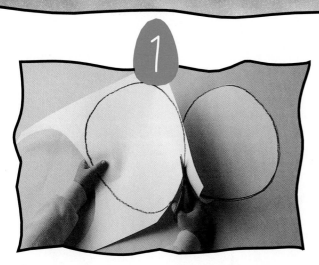

1

Cut out two egg shapes.

2

Draw a chick on one egg.

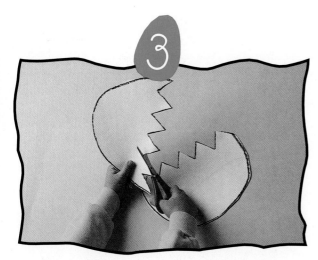

3

Cut the other in half.

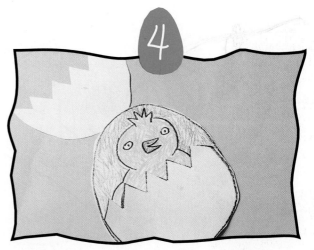

4

Tape one half at the top and bottom.

Use your hatching egg to tell about the chick that wouldn't hatch.

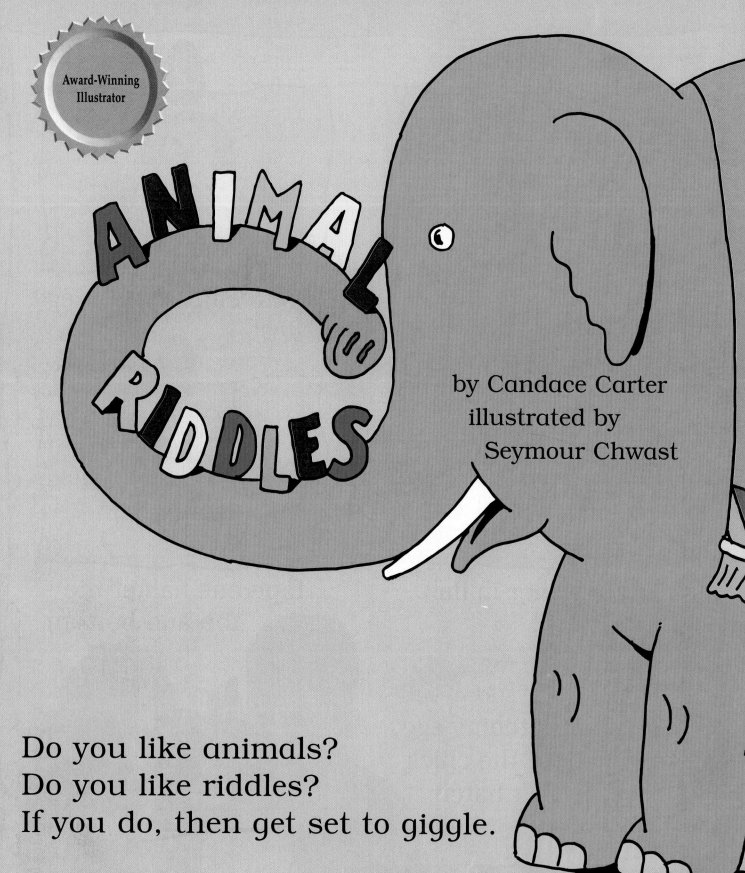

ANIMAL RIDDLES

by Candace Carter
illustrated by
Seymour Chwast

Do you like animals?
Do you like riddles?
If you do, then get set to giggle.

I am Dill, the Riddle Pickle.

My riddles will put a giggle in your middle!

30

Riddle 1

What animal can
you play ball with?

Hint
It has wings and can fly.

Answer
A bat!

Do you get it?
You can play
ball with a bat.
A bat is an
animal, too.

Riddle 2

What fish likes to drink milk?

Hint
Think of a pet that
laps up milk.

33

Answer
A catfish!

Riddle 3
What animal can tell time?

Hint
Think of things that tell the time.

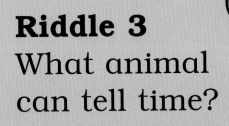

35

Answer
A watch dog.

Do you get it?
A watch tells the
time. A watch dog
is an animal!

Riddle 4
What does Dill do when his friends tickle him?

You know this one!

Answer
He giggles!

Wouldn't you?

Now it's time for YOU to think of some other riddles.

Share them with your friends and family!

39

Meet the Illustrator

SEYMOUR CHWAST

Seymour Chwast likes to draw funny, playful characters. His animals often act like people! He hopes you will find his drawings just as funny as the riddles. Seymour Chwast invites you to draw your own characters after reading *Animal Riddles*. Give it a try!

Seymour Chwast

Visit *The Learning Site!*
www.harcourtschool.com

41

RESPONSE ACTIVITY

RIDDLE

Make a flap book of riddles with classmates.

1 Why did the chicken cross the road ?

Write a riddle on a card.

2 Why did the chicken cross the road ?

Tape the card to a piece of paper.

3 To get to the other side.

Write the answer under the card.

4 Why did the chicken cross the road ?

Add some pictures.

BOOK ???

Put all the pages together to make a book.

Market Day

written by Carmen Parks
illustrated by Edward Martinez

Award-Winning
Illustrator

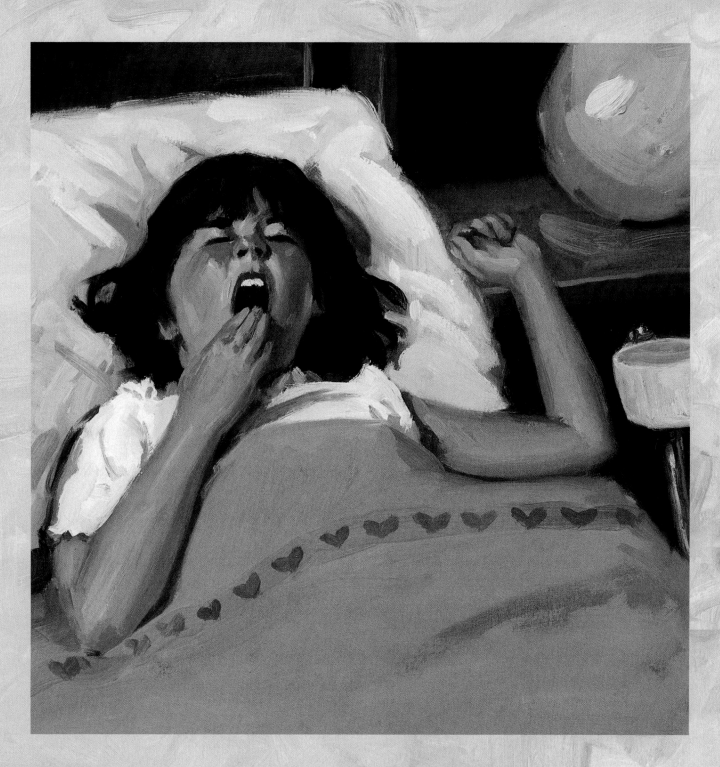

It's still dark, but it's time for me to get up. It's market day in Red Rock.

I always go to the market with
Mom and Dad. We sell lots of fruits
and vegetables from our farm.

As we start out this morning,
the stars are still out.

At last we get to Red Rock. We
park the truck in the big lot and
then set up our cart.

We have lots of fruits and
vegetables to sell.

"This corn smells fresh," a man says.
"These eggplants look fresh, too."

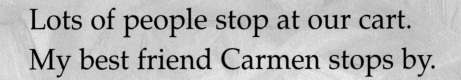

Lots of people stop at our cart.
My best friend Carmen stops by.

Carmen fills her arms with corn.
She gets some lemons, too.

Dad sells the last of the corn.
Nothing is left on the cart!

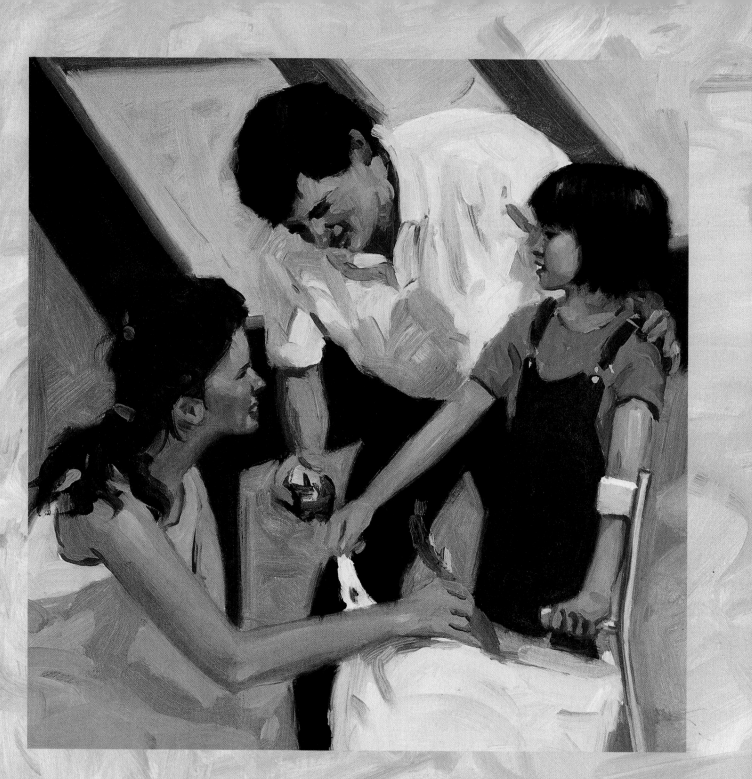

Market day is over. We pick up
the trash and go back home.

Market days always go by fast.
I think I like market days the best!

Visit *The Learning Site!*
www.harcourtschool.com

Edward Martinez

Ed Martinez loves to paint. He began his work on *Market Day* and *Carmen's Star* by taking pictures of real children. Then he looked at the photos as he painted the children in the stories. Carmen and her friends may be someone that you know!

Edward Martinez

Your Own Market

Make some foods to sell
at your own market.

1 Make some foods.

2 Make some price tags. Put them on the foods.

3 Take turns buying and selling the foods.

Award-Winning Illustrator

CARMEN'S STAR

written by Claire Daniel

illustrated by Ed Martinez

Carmen likes to make things.
One day she made a star with yarn.

Barb walked into the yard. "I like
that star. How did you make it?"
"I made it with yarn," said Carmen.

"Can I trade you my horse for that
star?" asked Barb. "I like it a lot!"
"Yes," said Carmen. "I like your
horse, too."

Barb saw Hector. "Where did you get that star?" asked Hector.
"I got it from Carmen," said Barb.

"Can I trade you this red cap for that star?" asked Hector.

"Yes," said Barb. "I want a red cap!"

Hector walked by Carmen's home
with the star. Carmen asked, "Is that
the yarn star I made?"

"Yes," said Hector. "I traded my red cap for it."

"Can I have it back?" asked Carmen.

"I would like to keep it," said Hector.

"I know!" said Hector. "We can help you make more stars.

"OK!" said Carmen.

"Let's start now," said Barb.

"We can make lots of stars to
give to friends!" said Carmen.

Here's how Carmen makes her stars.

72

Yesterday's Paper

Yesterday's paper makes a hat,
    Or a boat,
    Or a plane,
    Or a playhouse mat.
Yesterday's paper makes things
    Like that—
    And a very fine tent
    For a sleeping cat.

by Mabel Watts
illustrated by Marc Brown

RESPONSE ★ ACTIVITY

Twinkle Twinkle

Carmen and her friends enjoyed making yarn stars. Work with a group of classmates. Make up movements for the song "Twinkle, Twinkle, Little Star."

74

Twinkle, Twinkle, little star

How I wonder what you are

Up above the world so high

Like a diamond in the sky

Twinkle, Twinkle, little star

How I wonder what you are

MARCO'S RUN

Award-Winning Illustrator

WRITTEN BY WESLEY CARTIER
ILLUSTRATED BY REYNOLD RUFFINS

It's time for a run in the park. As I run,
I think, I must be fast. I wish I could
run like . . .

. . . a rabbit!

A rabbit hops through the grass.
He's kicking with his long back legs.
Off he goes.

I run like that rabbit. I hop and kick.
Then I think,

I must be fast. I wish I could run like . . .

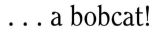

. . . a bobcat!

A bobcat runs on the forest path.
She darts off in a flash to hunt.

I run like that bobcat. I rush down
the park path. Then I think,

I must be very fast. I wish I could
run like . . .

. . . a horse!

A horse starts with a trot. Then, all of a sudden, she takes off like the wind!

I run like that horse. The wind swishes
past me. Then I think,

I must be the fastest of all.
I wish I could run like . . .

83

. . . a cheetah!

A swift cheetah flashes by. No one
can catch him!

I run like that cheetah.
Then,

I am huffing and puffing! I can't run
anymore. Now I wish I were . . .

. . . back home.

I huff and puff and sit down
with a thump.

Then I think,

NOW I NEED A REST!

Meet the Illustrator

REYNOLD RUFFINS

Reynold Ruffins loves to draw. He says, "Drawing can be a great adventure!" Drawing gives him the chance to show things that no one has ever thought of. "I like to show that pictures can tell a story just the way words do," he says.

Reynold Ruffins

Visit *The Learning Site!* www.harcourtschool.com

89

Animal Relay Races

Marco pretends to be a rabbit, a bobcat, a horse, and a cheetah. Now you can act like these animals in a relay race.

1 Line up in teams.

2 The first person hops like a rabbit to the finish line and back.

3 The second person crawls like a bobcat.

4 The third person trots like a horse.

5 The fourth person runs like a cheetah.

When everyone is
finished, you can REST
just like Marco!

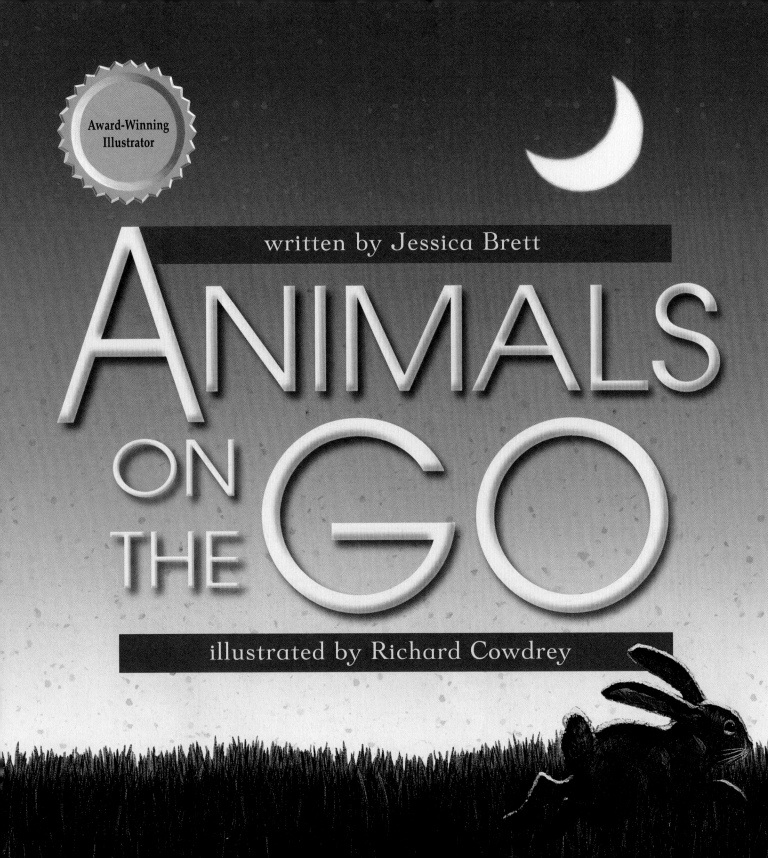

Award-Winning
Illustrator

written by Jessica Brett

ANIMALS
ON THE GO

illustrated by Richard Cowdrey

Zip! A mouse is little, but it's quick!
Animals must be quick to catch things
to eat. Read to find out about some
other fast animals.

Wild horses are on the go all the time.
If one horse sees danger, it lets the rest
know. Then they all run.

An ostrich is too big to fly, but it can
run very fast. An ostrich can run just
about as fast as a wild horse.

Rabbits are hunted by foxes and
bobcats. Rabbits run very fast as
they zig and zag through the grass.

If there is danger, a jackrabbit
thumps one leg. This lets the rest of
the jackrabbits know it's time to run.

Bobcats hunt at night. Even in
the dark, bobcats can see well.

When an animal comes—zap!
The bobcat runs fast to catch it.

A cheetah is the fastest animal that lives on land. It can even catch other fast animals.

A cheetah can run as fast as a car,
but not for long. In a short time, it
has to quit and take a rest.

Now you know about
some fast animals. Look
at the map to see where
these animals live.

Meet the Illustrator
RICHARD COWDREY

Richard Cowdrey draws pictures
for books, calendars, and posters.
He draws in a cabin by a pond in
the woods. Which animals do you
think Richard Cowdrey has seen
around his cabin?

105

RESPONSE ACTIVITY

ANIMAL

What is your favorite animal? Make an animal mask.

1 Draw the animal face on a paper plate.

2 Cut out holes for the eyes.

106

MASKS

3 Tape a stick to your mask.

4 Wear your mask. Tell a classmate what you know about your animal.

On the Way to the Pond

written by Angela Shelf Medearis

illustrated by Lorinda Bryan Cauley

One day, Tess Tiger went to visit
Vic Hippo. Vic packed a big basket
for a picnic at the pond.

"You bring the lunch," said Tess. "I'll
bring these very important things."
Vic just nodded.

They started up the path. It was a very
hot day. All of a sudden, Vic felt sick.

"Sit under my umbrella," said Tess.
"I'll fan you, too."

"Thanks," said Vic.

When Vic felt better they went off to the pond. All of a sudden, Vic stopped and cried, "Oh, no! I forgot the basket!"

"I'll go back and get it," said Tess.
"You go on."

Tess dropped some pebbles as she
walked. She found the picnic basket
and started back.

On the way, Tess stopped. She looked
this way and that way. She was lost!

"I know. I'll just follow these pebbles on the path."

Tess got to the pond, but she couldn't
find Vic. "Oh, no! Vic is lost!" She got
out her whistle. R-r-r-r!

"Here I am!" cried Vic. "I'm glad you had all that important stuff!"

"Yes," said Tess, "and I'm glad you packed a big lunch! I'm starving!"

Meet the Author
Angela Shelf Medearis

Angela Shelf Medearis loves to laugh and write silly stories. She has an office filled with toys. Her toys help give her ideas and make her laugh. She hopes that *On the Way to the Pond* puts a smile on your face.

Angela Shelf Medearis

Lorinda Bryan Cauley

**Visit *The Learning Site!*
www.harcourtschool.com**

120

Meet the Illustrator
Lorinda Bryan Cauley

It takes Lorinda Bryan Cauley about four days to draw the picture for one page of a book. First, she does pencil drawings. Then she adds color with colored pencils and colored ink.

Lorinda Bryan Cauley works very hard on the characters' eyes. She thinks the eyes are very important for showing feelings. What do you think?

Hippopotamus

Hello, I'm a big happy hippo,
I sleep in the sun till I'm hot,
And when I'm not sleeping
I mooch in the mud,
Which hippos like doing a lot.

by Giles Andreae
illustrated by David Wojtowycz

RESPONSE ✿ ACTIVITY

A Friendship Award

Tiger was a good friend to Hippo. Make an award for Tiger.

Tiger is a nice friend

Tiger helped hippo.

1
Trace a circle and ribbon.

2
Write something good about Tiger on the circle.

3
Write on the ribbon why Tiger is a good friend.

124

Tiger
is a
nice friend.

Tiger
helped
hippo.

Tiger
is a
nice friend.

Tiger
helped
hippo.

4

Glue the ribbon
to the circle.

5

Share your award.
Tell why Tiger is a
good friend.

125

I Wonder

Award-Winning
Author/
Photographer

story and photographs
by Tana Hoban

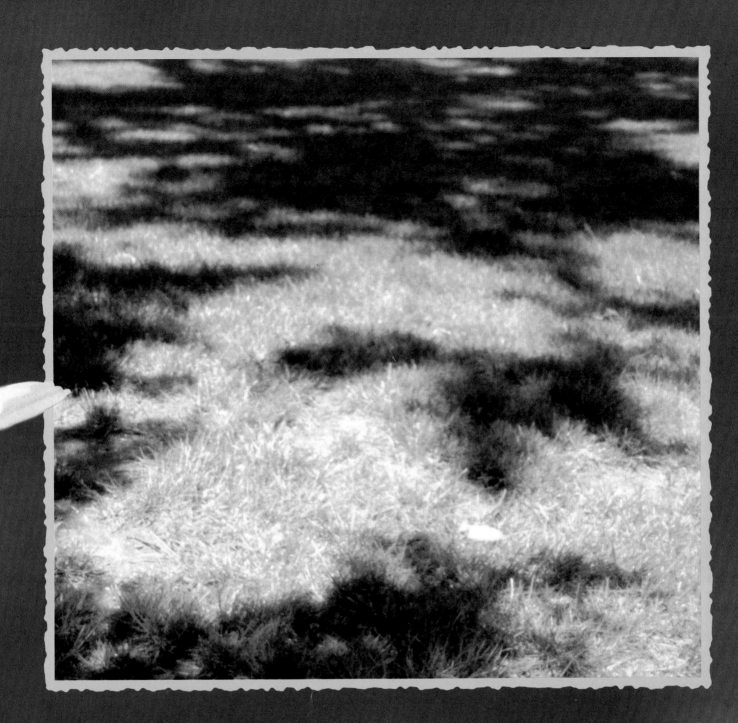

As I walk in the soft, green grass, I wonder about all the animals I see.

A caterpillar bumps and inches along.
Where did he come from?
Where is he going?

A cobweb sparkles in the morning sun.
Who spun it? Is it hard to spin a web?

Little bugs zip back and forth.
Are they happy or sad?
When they get home, will they be glad?

A robin is sitting high up on a branch.
Is he getting set to fly away?
Flying must be fun!

Who is that, buzz-buzzing from
blossom to blossom? Something
must smell sweet.

There's a zig-zag track in the mud.
Is this who came along with a
wiggle and a jiggle to make it?

A plump frog is sitting at the pond.
Will he jump in for a bath?
I think he will.

A duck paddles along with her ducklings. Are they all quacking

A kitten is playing in the grass.
Is he out for a walk, just like me?
I wish I could ask him.

As I walk back home, I wonder . . .
Do all the animals wonder
about me?

About the Author/Photographer

Tana Hoban

Tana Hoban takes a camera everywhere she goes. She is always looking for something new to take pictures of.

Tana Hoban took the pictures for *I Wonder* in Paris, France, where she lives. She hopes that they will help you see small things in a new way.

Tana Hoban

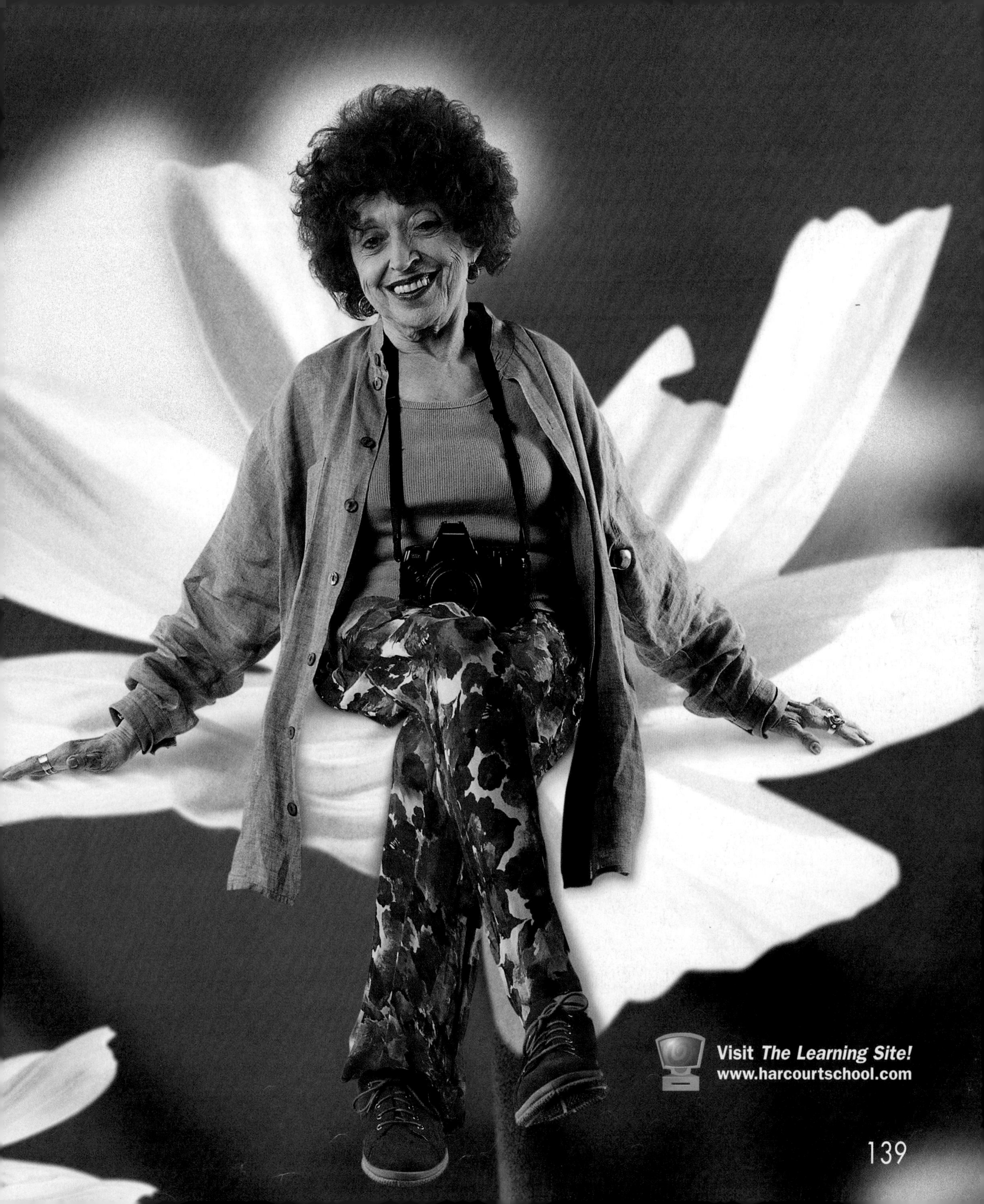

Visit *The Learning Site!*
www.harcourtschool.com

RESPONSE ACTIVITY

Your Own
Camera

Tana Hoban is a photographer.
You can be a photographer, too!

1 Fold a piece of paper in half. Tape the sides.

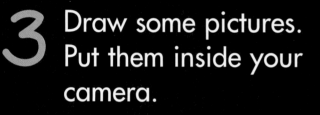

2 Make it look like a real camera.

3 Draw some pictures. Put them inside your camera.

4 "Develop" your film and share your pictures with classmates.

141

DIGGER PIG
✦ AND THE ✦
TURNIP

WRITTEN BY CARON LEE COHEN
ILLUSTRATED BY CHRISTOPHER DENISE

One day Digger Pig dug up a big
turnip. "I can use this to make a
good turnip pie," she said.

Chirper Chick, Quacker Duck, and Bow-Wow Dog sat around in their corner of the barn. "Let's make a turnip pie," said Digger Pig. "Who will help me cut the turnip?"

"Not I," said Chirper Chick.
"Not I," said Quacker Duck.
"Not I," said Bow-Wow Dog.

"All right then. I will cut the turnip myself."

And she did.

Then Digger Pig asked, "Who
will help me mash the turnip?"

"Not I," said Chirper Chick.

"Not I," said Quacker Duck.

"Not I," said Bow-Wow Dog.

"All right then. I will mash
the turnip myself."

And she did.

149

Next, Digger Pig asked,
"Who will help me make
the pie?"

"Not I," said Chirper Chick.
"Not I," said Quacker Duck.
"Not I," said Bow-Wow Dog.

"All right then. I will make
the pie myself!"

And she did.
She called her piglets to supper.

"Can we have some pie?" the
others asked.
"No!" grunted Digger Pig. "You
didn't help. My piglets and I
will eat it all."

And they did!

About the Author
CARON LEE COHEN

Caron Lee Cohen thinks of herself as a cook, like Digger Pig. She says that writing a story is a lot like preparing food. You have to mix together the right ingredients and then taste it to know the dish is just right!

Caron Lee Cohen

About the Illustrator
CHRISTOPHER DENISE

Christopher Denise

Christopher Denise likes drawing animals. Before he starts to draw, he looks at pictures of real animals to get ideas. He says, "I know children will like a story even more if the animals are really special."

 Visit *The Learning Site!* **www.harcourtschool.com**

155

Act It

Have a Digger Pig puppet show.

1 Draw Digger Pig and her friends. Cut them out.

2 Tape a craft stick to each puppet.

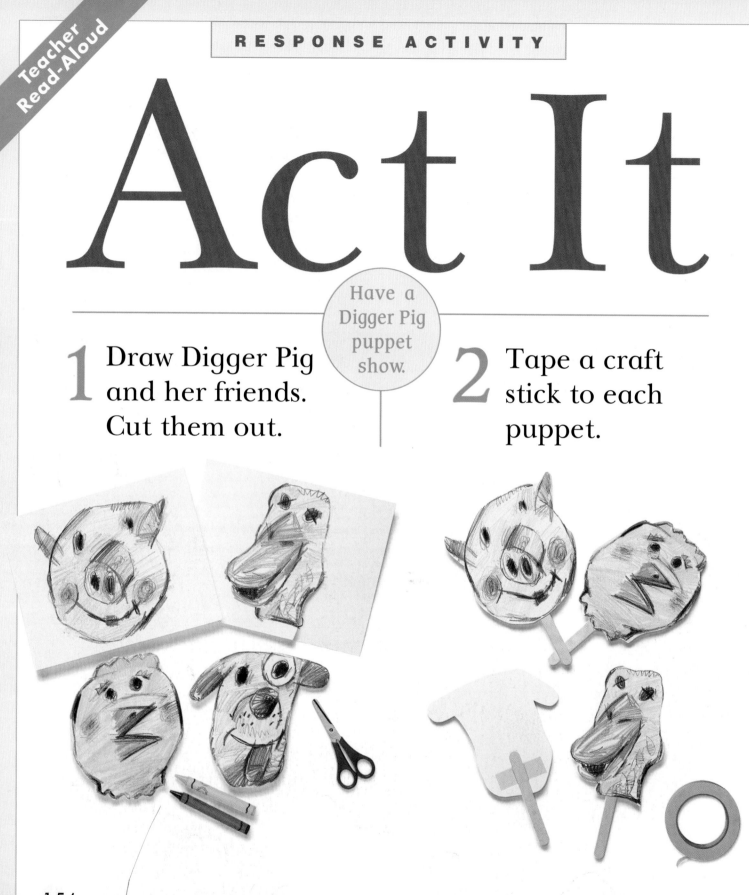

156

Out!

3 Think of new stories for Digger Pig and her friends.

4 Have a puppet show.

The Purple Snerd

written by Rozanne Lanczak Williams
illustrated by Mary GrandPré

One morning in March,
Fern was sitting outside.
Then all of a sudden . . .
"Snort! Chirp!" something cried.

It was under the porch.
Who or what could it be?
Some long purple fur
was all Fern could see.

It was smaller than her horse.
It was bigger than a bird.
Fern couldn't believe it—
could this be a Snerd?

The first thing Fern did
was to open her book.
Then she sat on a step
and had a good look.

Purple Snerds, the book said,
will purr, bark, and chirp.
When they eat their sweet snacks,
they will snort and slurp.

Curled under Fern's porch,
the thing chirped, barked, and purred.
It snorted and slurped
like a Purple Snerd!

It said, "Hello, Fern!"
"I'm so glad that we've met!
Can you find some sweet snacks—
as sweet as they get?"

"You're a Snerd!" cried Fern,
"Big and purple I see!
I saw Snerds in my book
and now one's here with me!"

Fern and the Snerd
played around and had fun.
They even played Snerdball
outside in the sun!

Their time went by fast,
and the Snerd had to go.
"So long, Fern," he chirped.
"I'll come back, you know."

"So long," called Fern.
"It was such a fun day.
Bring more Purple Snerds
to my house to play!"

Meet the Author

Rozanne Lanczak Williams

Where do you get ideas for your stories?

I keep a notebook with me all the time. I write down my thoughts and ideas. When I need an idea for a story, I look in my notebook.

Why do you like to write for children?

I think children learn to write from what they read. After you read "The Purple Snerd" you may want to write and tell your own stories.

Visit *The Learning Site!*
www.harcourtschool.com

170

Mary Grand Pré

Rozanne Lanczak Williams

Meet the Illustrator

Mary Grand Pré

How did you decide how to draw the Purple Snerd?

When I was thinking about the Purple Snerd, I saw my dog.
Charlie has a hairy face and loves to eat sweets. Somehow,
the Purple Snerd turned out to look a lot like Charlie!

What other things do you like to do besides drawing?

I like to visit schools to talk to children about my work.
I show them how to draw things.

171

COLOR FUN!

Did you know that blue and red make the color purple? Mix these colors and see for yourself.

The Orange Slurp Gets Lost

An orange slurp got lost one day. He was sad. He was afraid. I found him and took him to his mother. Now we are friends.

1 Mix two other colors to make a new color.

2 Paint a character. Name it when finished.

3 Write a story about it. Share it with classmates.

The
Fox
and the
Stork

retold and illustrated by
Gerald McDermott

Long ago there was a fox who lived
in the forest. Fox liked to play tricks
on his friends.

One morning, Fox rowed his boat
around the pond. He saw his friend
Stork. "Would you like to come to
my house for dinner?" Fox asked.

"How kind of you to ask!" said
Stork. "Yes. I would like that."

The next day, Stork went to Fox's
house for dinner. She tapped on
Fox's door with her long bill.

"Come in," said Fox. "I made soup!"

"Wonderful!" said Stork. "I like soup."

Fox and Stork sat down to eat. Fox didn't put the soup in a bowl. He served it in a flat dish.

Fox felt very smart. Stork couldn't eat
from the flat dish. All she could do was
dip the tip of her long bill into the soup.
Fox soon slurped it all up!

Stork was still hungry, but she didn't complain.

"Thank you for the dinner," said Stork. "Come to my house, and I'll make dinner for you."

The next day, Fox rowed his boat to Stork's house.

"I don't like to boast," said Stork,
"but my soup is the best. I use
greens that grow in my own garden."

"Wonderful!" said Fox. "Let's eat!"

Stork served the soup in a tall
jar. Fox couldn't get a drop. All
he could do was lick the top of
the jar. Stork dipped in her long
bill and drank it all up.

Fox moaned and groaned as
he rowed home.

"I'm so hungry! This is my
reward for tricking a friend!"

At last Fox saw that being kind
to others is the right thing to do.

Meet the Author/Illustrator

Gerald McDermott

Visit *The Learning Site!*
www.harcourtschool.com

Gerald McDermott likes to retell fables and folktales because these stories have important messages. He uses his pictures to help tell the story and relate the message to his readers. Gerald McDermott hopes that you enjoy *The Fox and the Stork.*

Be My Guest

Fox and Stork invited each other to dinner.
Pretend that you are the fox or
the stork. Make a dinner invitation.

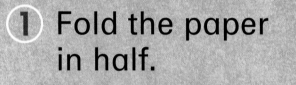

1 Fold the paper in half.

2 Write the invitation.

What: Dinner
Where: Fox's house
Time: 6:00 PM
Please Come!

3 Draw a picture on the front.

4 Give your invitation to a friend.

Have a pretend dinner and act out the Fox and Stork story.

The Very Boastful Kangaroo

by Bernard Most

Award-Winning
Author/Illustrator

Skip Kangaroo was a very boastful fellow.
"I can jump higher than any kangaroo," he
bragged. "I am the best jumper of all!"

Just then, some of Skip's friends hopped by. "Let's have a jumping contest," said a little kangaroo. "The one who jumps highest will win."

Skip chuckled. "I can jump much, much higher than anyone. I'll win the contest because I'm the best jumper of all!"

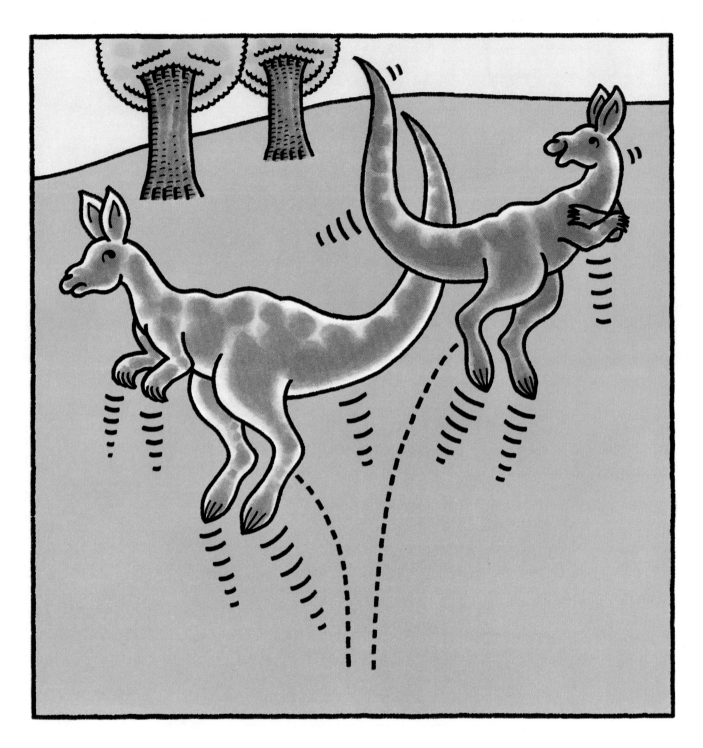

The first kangaroo jumped high, but Skip
jumped higher. "See?" Skip bragged.

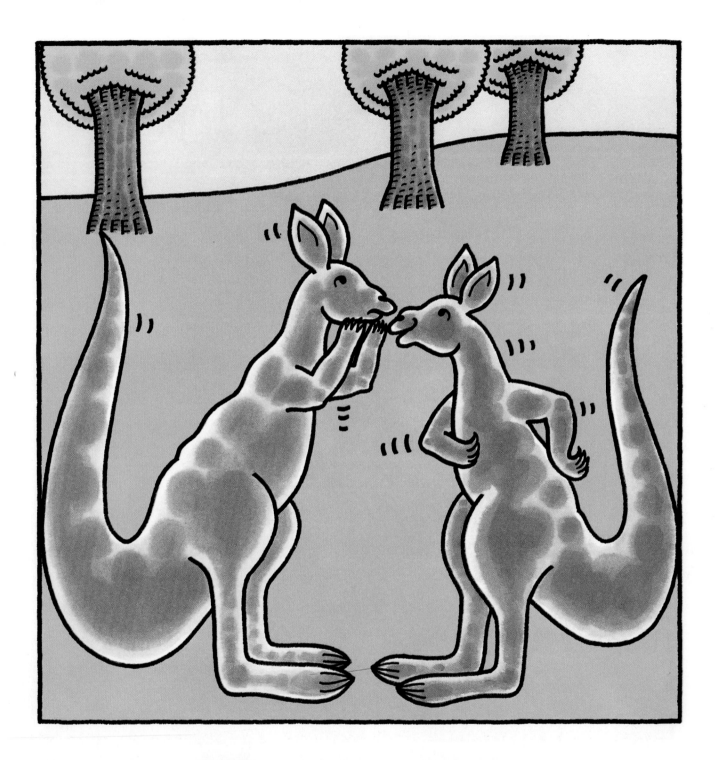

The first kangaroo just groaned.
"Who is next?" asked Skip.

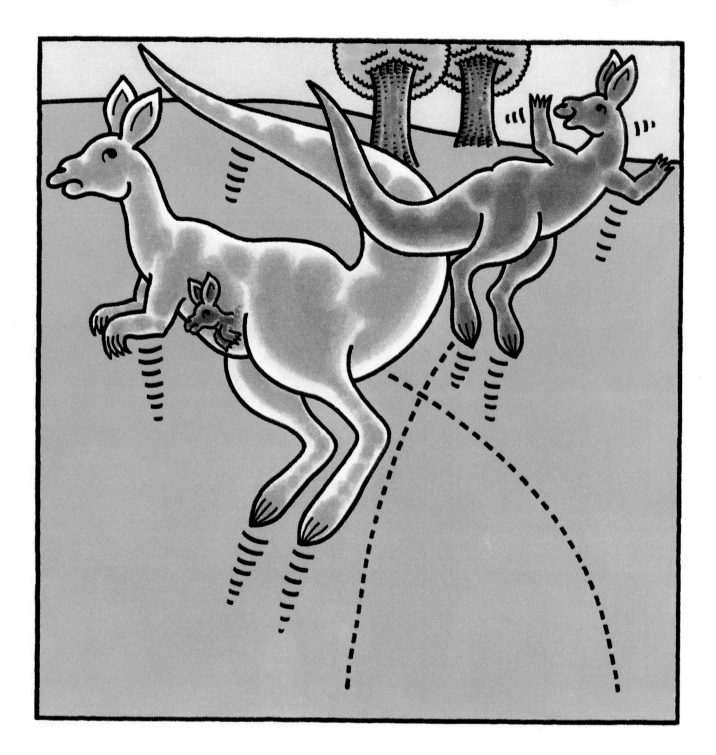

The next kangaroo jumped very high, but Skip
jumped higher. "I'm a star!" Skip bragged.

All the other kangaroos just moaned.
"I showed you!" bragged Skip. "I win!
I'm the best! I win the contest!"

"Not yet!" called Baby Joey. "It's my turn!
Can you jump higher than that oak tree?"

"That oak tree?" asked Skip. "That tree is much, much too tall. I'm the best jumper of all, but even I can't jump that high."

"Well," said Baby Joey, "if I can jump higher than that tall oak tree, will I win the contest?"

"Yes," Skip chuckled, "but you will never,
ever do it! No one can jump that high!"

Baby Joey jumped a baby jump. Then he
shouted, "I win! I win the jumping contest. . .

. . . BECAUSE TREES CAN'T JUMP!"
Everyone had a very good, very long giggle—
even Skip. (He giggled the longest of all!)

Meet the Author/Illustrator

Bernard Most

Bernard Most has his characters find interesting ways to solve their problems. In *The Very Boastful Kangaroo*, Baby Joey finds a clever way to win the jumping contest. The author wants his readers to know that even though they are small, they can do anything they want if they just try. Bernard Most always tells children to follow their dreams and says, "Never give up!"

Bernard Most

206

Visit *The Learning Site!*
www.harcourtschool.com

Pocket Protectors

Baby kangaroos
are called joeys.
At first, a joey
stays in its mom's
pocket all the time.

Later, it will go
in and out.
Mom's pocket is
safe and warm.

RESPONSE ACTIVITY

If You're Happy and You Know It

All the kangaroos were happy
that Baby Joey tricked Skip.
Join them in the song

"If You're Happy and
You Know It."

210

If you're happy and you know it,
clap your hands.

If you're happy and you know it,
clap your hands.

If you're happy and you know it,
then you'll really want to
show it.

If you're happy and you
know it, clap your hands.

Acknowledgments

For permission to reprint copyrighted material, grateful acknowledgment is made to the following sources:

Patricia Babcock, on behalf of Mabel Watts: "Yesterday's Paper" by Mabel Watts.

Henry Holt and Company, Inc.: Cover illustration from *Mr. Gumpy's Outing* by John Burningham. Copyright © 1970 by John Burningham.

Alfred A. Knopf, Inc.: Illustration by Marc Brown from *Read-Aloud Rhymes for the Very Young,* selected by Jack Prelutsky. Illustration copyright © 1986 by Marc Brown.

Little Tiger Press: "Hippopotamus" from *Rumble in the Jungle* by Giles Andreae, illustrated by David Wojtowycz. Text © 1996 by Giles Andreae; illustrations © 1996 by David Wojtowycz.

National Wildlife Federation: "Pocket Protectors" from *Your Big Backyard* Magazine, March 1998. Text copyright 1998 by the National Wildlife Federation.

Photo Credits

Key: (T)=top, (B)=bottom, (C)=center, (L)=left, (R)=right

Michael Campos Photography, 26, 27, 42, 43, 59, 75, 91, 106, 107, 124, 125, 140, 141, 156, 157; Mike Woodside, 171; Michael Campos Photography, 172, 173, 190, 191; John Cancalosi/Peter Arnold, Inc., 208

All other photos by Harcourt Brace:

Chuck Kneyse/Black Star; Walt Chyrnwski/Black Star; Rick Falco/Black Star; Tom Sobolik/Black Star; Larry Hamill/Black Star; Anna Clopet/Black Star; Rick Friedman/Black Star; Peter Stone/Black Star; Todd Bigelow/Black Star; Kevin Delahunty/Black Star

Illustration Credits

Gerald McDermott, Cover Art; Gary Taxali, 4-11; Lisa Campbell Ernst, 12-25; Tracy Sabin, 26-27, 74-75, 90-91, 124-125, 140-141, 172-173, 190-191; Seymour Chwast, 28-43; Edward Martinez, 44-71; Marc Brown, 72-73; Reynold Ruffins, 76-89; Richard Cowdrey, 92-107; Lorinda Bryan Cauley, 108-121; David Wojtowycz, 122-123; Christopher Denise, 142-155; George Kreif, 156-157; Mary GrandPré, 158-171; Gerald McDermott, 174-190; Bernard Most, 192-207, 210-211